Edited by **Mark Derosier**
Illustrated by **Aissa Mutiara Putri**

Sabine Ruh House is teaming up with the heroes at World Animal
Protection and The Sloth Conservation Foundation for this special
book. Each purchase not only opens a world of understanding
for children, but also contributes to World Animal Protection's
essential work in wildlife conservation. It's a small step from you,
but it means the world to the animals that these organizations
tirelessly work to protect.

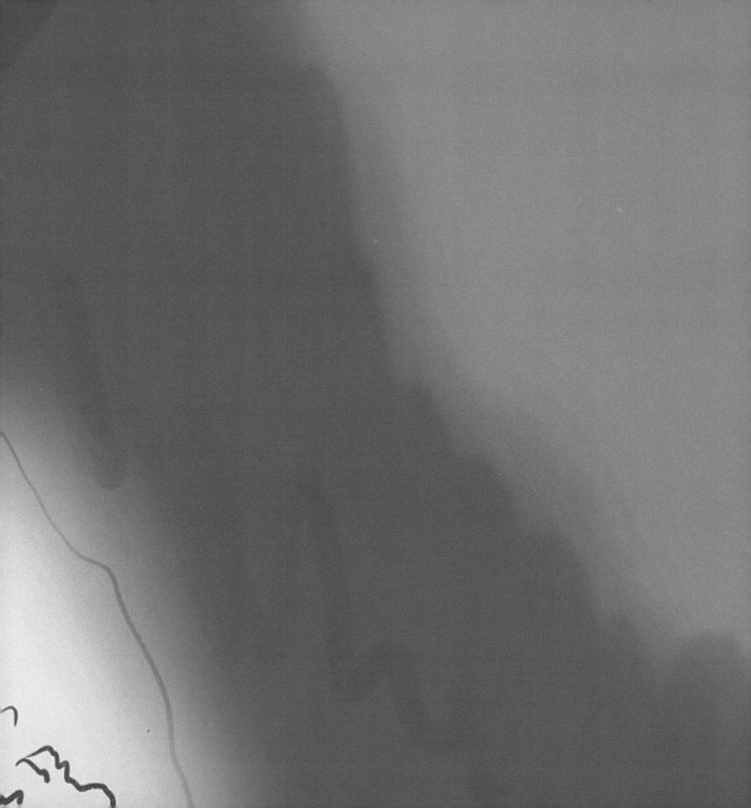

Introduction:

Welcome, young reader, to an enchanting world that will gently guide you along the path of empathy, acceptance, and love. As you journey through the pages of "Learning to Love Stevie," we invite you to open your heart and mind to the beauty of diversity, the strength of friendship, and the importance of protecting our fellow creatures in the wild.

"Learning to Love Stevie" is a poetic tribute to the extraordinary. Here, you will meet Stevie, a remarkable sloth who may move slowly but teaches us invaluable life lessons of resilience, patience, and adaptation. Stevie's story is more than just an entertaining narrative; it is a journey towards understanding and accepting the unique qualities that each of us, and the animals we share this planet with, possess.

As you delight in the adventures of Stevie, take a moment to reflect on the real-life counterparts of our sloth friend. In the rainforests of Central and South America, sloths lead an existence that is a testament to nature's ingenuity - conserving energy, mastering camouflage, exhibiting unexpected strength, and even swimming with surprising speed. Yet, it's crucial to remember that sloths, like many of our planet's wonderful creatures, are best appreciated in their natural habitats.

By taking this journey, you also join a much larger movement – one that stands for wildlife protection, the celebration of diversity, and the fostering of empathy. We present scientific references that underpin the themes of our story, each a testament to the significance of fostering emotional intelligence, developing social competence, and conserving biodiversity. Together, these elements contribute to a holistic approach to child development and environmental stewardship.

Engage with the activities that further deepen your understanding of these themes. Imagine your adventures with Stevie, learn about real-world sloths, and explore ways you can contribute to wildlife protection. We hope this leads to intriguing conversations, inspired creativity, and meaningful action.

As you flip through these pages, remember, every word is a step towards a broader understanding of our diverse world. Each illustration is a window into a realm where acceptance and empathy reign. And every verse, a call to embrace uniqueness, whether in ourselves, in others, or the wildlife we share our planet with.

Welcome to the world of "Learning to Love Stevie" – a world that celebrates diversity, champions wildlife protection, and cherishes friendships. Enjoy this delightful journey of discovery and may the insights you gain from this book resonate far beyond its pages.

Learning to Love

Stevie

In proud collaboration with World Animal Protection and The Sloth Conservation Foundation

by Sabine Ruh House

Ann and Stevie
Were thick as thieves
But not without
Their pet peeves!

Like the wind ran, Ann
Quick as lightning,
Swift as a swan, was she

While Stevie did dawdle
He moseyed by –
His saunter serene,
He'd wander at peace,
Meander did he
With no zest or worries

Stevie really had
Nothing to prove,
For even though
He hardly did move
His tales remain
Widely known –
Here's one now,
Don't read it alone!

Stevie did not pantomime,
But if time was money
He would surely take
Your every last dime.

In vim and vigor
Stevie did not train
He saved his strength
For when it might rain.

Time did crawl
When he had his way,
For he did drift -
Welcoming no haste
He'd simply embrace
His leisurely pace.

Ann and Stevie
Were thick as thieves
But not without
Their pet peeves!

This one time,
In particular, I recall,
We took a trip
To the nearest mall

I was there to buy
Mother a comfy shawl,
But Stevie had his eye
On this fancy toy.

So, to Toyland we went,
To his greatest joy,
But to my dismay,
And absolute shock,
We stood there a month
To pay for this purchase small!

Ann and Stevie
Were thick as thieves
But not without
Their pet peeves!

Maybe he was asked
To go-fly-a-kite,
Or maybe he just
Loved playing the clown

Because every so often
While we all walked upright,
This gentle wise guy
Would swing upside-down.

Ann and Stevie
Were thick as thieves
But not without
Their pet peeves!

Stevie struck a clever deal
With the very green algae,
And let the moss grow
On his coat – so crafty!
Stevie wasn't shallow, just canny,
He loved them, and they loved he.

When eagles swooped
And Jaguars prowled,
Tummies empty
Loudly growled,
Stevie put on his
Bright green coat,
Pretending now
To be a shrub unseen.

I set out to tell you
This very story
Of how I learned
To love Stevie.
Sure, I could move
Faster than he –
But he had the smarts
To live in the wild free.

Stevie was strong,
When he had to flee,
Especially in water,

He was strong times three!
I wouldn't say it
If it wasn't true
But he could out-swim me
And probably you, too!

Stevie was an expert diver
He could hold his breath
For half an hour
You and I would
Rattle and rasp,
Pant and gasp,
Oh, we would not
Cease to wheeze –
Our little faces
Would go blue,
Free water diving
is hardly a breeze!

So next time your friend
Does loudly chew,
Or does something funny
You'd never dream to do,
Think of Stevie and his
Extraordinary ways,
His quirks make him special
Just like me and you

For Ann and Stevie
Were thick as thieves
And ended up making
Wonderful memories!

About the Poem:

"Learning to Love Stevie" is a heartfelt and entertaining exploration of friendship, empathy, and understanding. This delightful story unravels the strength of acceptance, the beauty of diversity, and the importance of recognizing and appreciating each other's unique qualities. The poem aims to inspire young readers to nurture strong bonds, foster inclusivity, and respect the fascinating world of wildlife.

Learning from Sloths:

Sloths are truly wondrous creatures. These tree-dwelling tropical mammals from Central and South America have unique adaptations that make them remarkably efficient and impressively strong. Sloths conserve energy with their efficient metabolism, skillfully blend into the rainforest with their unique fur that fosters over 80 types of algae and fungi, and display amazing strength, with grip power three times stronger than the average human. They even outperform their terrestrial movement speed in water, swimming three times faster! Learn more about these fantastic creatures at The Sloth Conservation Foundation (**https://slothconservation.org/**).

While we adore the imaginary Stevie, it's crucial to remember that real-world sloths belong in the wild. You can help protect sloths and other wild animals by not buying them as pets.

Supporting Wildlife Protection:

"Learning to Love Stevie" proudly collaborates with World Animal Protection, a global non-profit organization that exposes and rectifies exploitative and cruel systems. World Animal Protection has been rewriting the story for animals for over 70 years and prioritizes animals in farming and wild animals exploited for entertainment, pets, and fashion.

Scientific References:

"Cultural Diversity and Children's Empathy: The Role of Maternal Conversations about Race" by Cheah et al. (2018) explores how conversations about respect for and understanding of racial out-groups can foster empathy in children. Similarly, the poem speaks to the acceptance of others' unique characteristics and actions, emphasizing the development of empathy towards diverse beings - in this case, a sloth named Stevie.

"Intercultural Competence Development in Pupils: A Multilevel Perspective" by Gross and Melkman (2021) focuses on the development of intercultural competence, which includes emotional intelligence. This theme resonates with the poem as Ann develops emotional intelligence through her interaction with Stevie, learning to appreciate and understand his slow pace and unique habits.

"Wildlife Conservation and Animal Welfare: Two Sides of the Same Coin?" by Baker et al. (2019) presents the idea that successful wildlife conservation efforts should consider animal welfare issues. This ties into the poem as it not only introduces the reader to the unique behavior and survival tactics of sloths but also promotes the idea of wildlife protection and respect for animals in their natural habitats. Stevie's representation as a creature of the wild who should be appreciated but not removed from his environment echoes the paper's themes.

"Sloths Like It Hot: Ambient Temperature Modulates Food Intake in the Brown-Throated Sloth (Bradypus variegatus)" by Cliffe and Avey-Arroyo (2015) directly pertains to the wildlife theme of the poem. It provides a real-world scientific context to the behavior and adaptations of sloths, like Stevie, enhancing the understanding and appreciation of these fascinating creatures, which is a central theme in the poem.

Activity Ideas:

1. Discuss the unique qualities of Stevie the sloth and what we can learn from them.

2. Create a story about an adventure that Ann and Stevie could go on together.

3. Download a free kid's activity book to learn more about how to protect wild animals.

Further Resources: If you're interested in learning more about sloths, check out The Sloth Conservation Foundation's website at **https://slothconservation.org/**. Remember, although Stevie is a wonderful and fun character in this book, real-world sloths are wild animals and belong in the wild. You can help protect sloths and other wild animals by not buying wild animals as pets.

World Animal Protection is a global nonprofit organization that works tirelessly to protect animals worldwide. For over 70 years, they have been rewriting the story for animals, working to expose and combat harmful practices. Visit **https://www.worldanimalprotection.us/** to learn more about their incredible work.

Remember, just like Ann learned to appreciate Stevie's unique way of life, we should strive to appreciate and celebrate the diverse world around us. Each of us has a part to play in promoting acceptance and inclusion.

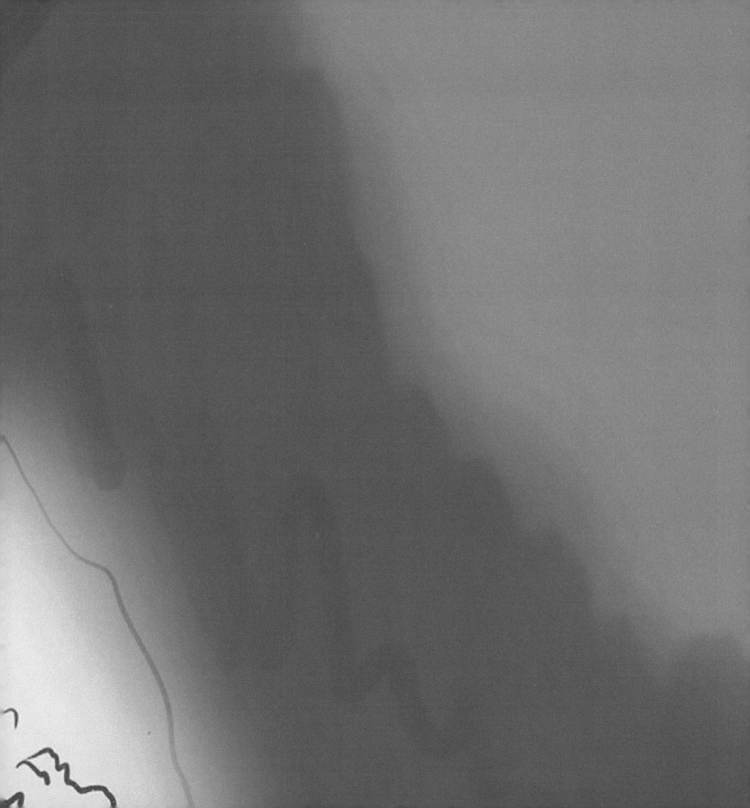

Printed in the USA
CPSIA information can be obtained
at www.ICGtesting.com
LVHW071950011123
762649LV00020B/814